A Different Kind of Dog

Written by **Linda and Frank Sebenius**

Illustrated by **Sherrill Hull**

We would like to dedicate this book to Sherrill's big brother Owen, who loved animals and instilled such playfulness in her. Thanks for watching over her and helping to create such a wonderful partner in this endeavor.

— *Linda and Frank Sebenius*

A Different Kind of Dog
WRITERS: Linda and Frank Sebenius
ILLUSTRATOR: Sherrill Hull
PUBLISHER: The BooneDoggies, LLC

Library of Congress Cataloging in Publication Data
Sebenius, Frank 1956 -
Sebenius, Linda 1958 -
Hull, Sherrill 1946 -
A Different Kind of Dog
    SUMMARY: Boone, a very unusual looking dachshund, shows how all of his dachshund family may look different, but many things are the same, and being different is what makes them special.
    (1. Dachshunds - Fiction.   2. Dogs - Fiction)
1. Title.
ISBN: 978-0-9905482-0-1

Printed in South Korea

Requests for permission should be addressed in writing to:
The BooneDoggies, LLC
PO Box 124
Duvall, Washington 98019

Hi there. My name is Boone.

I'm a different kind of dog.

2

Daddy and Mommy are different kinds of dogs too.

Oh, my whole family is the same kind of dog.
We are called Dachshunds.

It sounds like "duck sounds" when you say it.

We are sometimes called wiener dogs or hotdogs because we are long and have short legs.

A real fun thing about dachshunds is that they come in all sorts of colors and hair styles.

My Mommy has long curly hair that is blond,
brown and black all at the same time. Her name is Sonya.

My Daddy has beautiful long cream colored hair
and a big bushy tail. His name is Gus.

My hair is long, white and fluffy. I have very big feet.
I am small, but I am big!

My brother and sister have different hair too. Leana has long, black and cream colored hair that is curly like Mommy's.

Flynn has hair that looks just like Daddy's, but his is reddish brown.

Flynn loves to eat. Anything and everything!

Auntie Piper's hair is long, black and tan.
She teaches us good manners.

We all may look different on the outside,
but guess what?

There are still a lot of things that are the same!

We all like to dig.

We all like to chase butterflies.

We all like to snuggle.

But being different…

That is what makes us special!

The Ends

Parent Guide
Page-by-Page Ideas

I'm a Different Kind of Dog: P 2 / 3
Two dogs look a lot alike. Can you find them?
Where is the Cat?
Can you find Boone?
How many clouds do you see?

Dad and Mom: P 4
Which dog house name is the same spelled forwards and backwards?

Duck Sounds: P 5
Who is the author of the book they are reading?
Can you find the snail?
How many yellow daffodils do you see? How many more flowers do you see?
What is the duck saying?

Eat Not to Eat: P 6
One of the letters is missing on Flynn's bib. What do you think it says?
What is the word around his plate?

Sonya: P 8
Who wrote the book Sonya is reading? What is the Title of the book?
What is the name of the Dog Groomer?

Gus: P 9
What does it say around the mirror?
How many brushes does Gus have? How many combs?

Boone: P 10
The number on this page is 3. Why? Or is it 4?
Is it easy for Boone to run in these shoes?

Leana: P 11
What is your favorite ribbon? Stripes, polkadots, or a solid color?
What do you think is in the bottle on the shelf? A genie? Perfume? A magic potion? Or?
Which one of the hanging things would Leana need to go for a walk?

Flynn: P 12
What does the picture say on the wall? How about the sign above the shelves?
Can you find all 4 bowls of food on this page?

Auntie Piper: P 13
What time is it?
What do the students call the teacher?
What is sitting on the end of Auntie Piper's nose?
What are some manners that GOOD dogs DO?

We all like to dig: P 15
Why is the duck holding an umbrella?
Where is Auntie Piper? Which one is Boone? Flynn? Leana? Sonya? Gus?
How many flowers do you see? How many bones?

Chasing Butterflies: P 16 / 17
How many butterflies do you see? Snails? Bees?
Which dog has all four feet on the ground? Which one has three?

Snuggle: P 18
Which slipper does not have a match?
Who is sleeping inside the hole in the wall?
What does the sign say on the wall?
How many bones do you see? How many balls? Slippers?

Being Different: P 19
How are they different? How are they the same?

At the Door: P 20
Which is which?

For more information on how to use this book for school readiness, visit
www.TheBooneDoggies.com